LOVE VOLTAIRE US APART

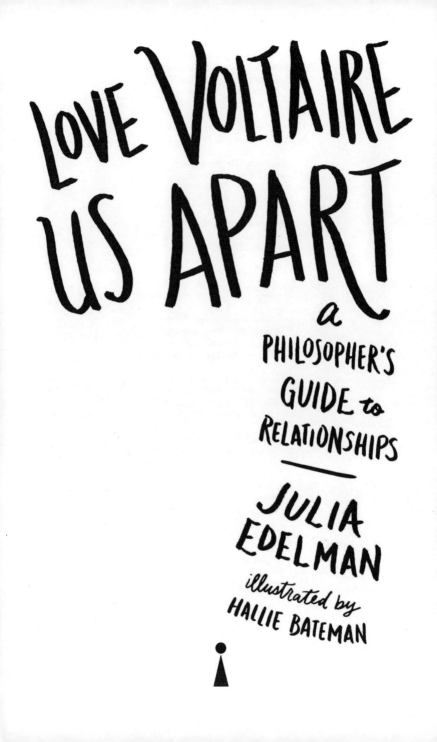

LOVE VOLTAIRE US APART

a PHILOSOPHER'S GUIDE to RELATIONSHIPS

JULIA EDELMAN

illustrated by HALLIE BATEMAN

First published in the UK in 2016 by
Icon Books Ltd, Omnibus Business Centre,
39–41 North Road, London N7 9DP
email: info@iconbooks.com
www.iconbooks.com

This edition published in the UK in 2017
and in the USA in 2018 by Icon Books

Sold in the UK, Europe and Asia
by Faber & Faber Ltd, Bloomsbury House,
74–77 Great Russell Street,
London WC1B 3DA or their agents

Distributed in the UK, Europe and Asia
by Grantham Book Services, Trent Road,
Grantham NG31 7XQ

Distributed in the USA by
Publishers Group West,
1700 Fourth Street, Berkeley, CA 94710

Distributed in Canada by
Publishers Group Canada,
76 Stafford Street, Unit 300
Toronto, Ontario M6J 2S1

Distributed in Australia and New Zealand
by Allen & Unwin Pty Ltd,
PO Box 8500, 83 Alexander Street,
Crows Nest, NSW 2065

Distributed in South Africa by
Jonathan Ball, Office B4, The District,
41 Sir Lowry Road, Woodstock 7925

Distributed in India by Penguin Books India,
7th Floor, Infinity Tower – C, DLF Cyber City,
Gurgaon 122002, Haryana

ISBN: 978-178578-224-4

Typeset and designed by Simmons Pugh
Printed and bound in the UK by Clays Ltd, St Ives plc

For my family

About the Author

Julia Edelman grew up in New York. She studied film theory and philosophy at McGill University. Her work has appeared in *The New Yorker*, *New York* magazine, *McSweeney's Internet Tendency*, *VICE*, *Cosmopolitan*, *Playboy*, *CollegeHumor*, and the *Believer*. She lives in Brooklyn.

About the Illustrator

Hallie Bateman is a Los Angeles-based writer and illustrator. Her work can be seen on halliebateman.com

"Kant would have been one of the greatest phenomena of mankind in general if he had been able to feel love."

Ernst Cassirer, *Kant's Life and Thought*

Contents

Introduction

This is the only book you'll ever need. You can use it as a self-defence weapon (the pages are razor-sharp), a way to carry snacks to your room when you've run out of plates, or a face shield for when you see your ex-dentist on the street because you still feel bad, but know moving on was for the best.

If you eventually decide to open this book, however, you'll find that there are words and illustrations you might enjoy!

I am a writer and comedian from New York, but began this book when I was living in Montreal. It was the dead of winter, and I continued to write only because my rough drafts fed the fire that allowed me to survive. At the time, I was studying philosophy and while I should have been finishing essays for class, found myself writing about philosophers' love lives instead. I liked thinking about Nietzsche's best pickup lines, or what Jean-Paul Sartre and Simone de Beauvoir's breakup was like—and then I got the chance to turn these thoughts into a book.

If you're reading this, you are either trying to impress someone in your Marx study group, or want to give your partner a gift that says: "Hey, I'm into you, and I feel like you *also* stay awake at night thinking about how small and insignificant we are in this ever-expanding universe." Maybe your heart is broken because your lover ran off to write a manifesto, and you could use some advice for this very relatable situation. If none of the above applies, you might just be afraid of ending up like Kant. Don't worry, we all are.

Falling
in Love

Famous Quotes, Explained

History finally starts to make some sense

There is always some madness in love. But there is also always some reason in madness.
Nietzsche (*Thus Spoke Zarathustra*, 1891)

Nietzsche said this famous line after finally figuring out how to put together a bed frame from IKEA.

Love is composed of a single soul inhabiting two bodies.
Aristotle (Plato's *Symposium*, c. 385–370BC)

Aristotle wrote this at a time when he wasn't quite ready to move in with his boyfriend just yet, even though he had been hinting about it for months. They were a single soul, sure, but inhabiting two bodies, and hopefully in two separate apartments.

Love is a canvas furnished by nature and embroidered by imagination.
Voltaire (1694–1778)

Voltaire mumbled these famous words while getting very drunk at his first Paint Nite.

At the touch of love everyone becomes a poet.
Plato (428–347BC)

Plato wrote this while lamenting his lover's recent interest in slam poetry.

To fear love is to fear life, and those who fear life are already three parts dead.
Bertrand Russell (*Marriage and Morals*, 1929)

Russell realized he was three parts dead when he found himself running away from home. He loved his wife, but didn't want to explain why he forgot to take out the garbage again.

The meeting of two personalities is like the contact of two chemical substances: if there is any reaction, both are transformed.
Carl Jung (1875–1961)

Jung used this line to defend himself after having an affair. He didn't *want* to sleep with his patient, but he couldn't deny their chemistry, either.

I swear by my life and my love of it that I will never live for the sake of another man, nor ask another man to live for mine.
Ayn Rand (*Atlas Shrugged*, 1957)

Rand spoke these words when reciting her wedding vows. No one was sure whether they were supposed to clap or not.

One word frees us of all the weight and pain in life. That word is Love.
Sophocles (496–406BC)

Sophocles was trying to give a friend advice, but it turned out that "love" does not cure cholera.

Love Letters

Philosophers abandon papers for pickup lines

♡

The only thing I know is that I know nothing. We've gathered at the agora several times and discussed our shared regard for divinity, but I hardly know anything about you! Have you always been a midwife? Would you pursue virtue over material wealth? How many siblings do you have? I am ignorant of many things, but I do know something about the art of love: it's just asking a lot of questions until the other person is too tired to go on! Shall I continue?

Socrates

♡

♡

Before we met, I was trapped deep within a cave, and had no way out. But you were my light, and led me out of the darkness. I'd love if the two of us could leave the cave sometime and embrace our enlightened selves over dinner. My good friend, Diogenes, is playing his harp at the first set of the sun later if you'd like to join me.

Plato

♡

♡

It seems to me that it is essential to eliminate doubt and determine certainty. So, I must ask: when I watched you prepare Queen Christina of Sweden's robes, and you looked back at me, was that an I-could-be-interested kind of look, or did you just have something in your eye? I'll understand if you do not wish to respond. Uncertainty is the only true certainty, after all.

Descartes

♡

I must admit, your support for women's rights is quite arousing.* It's that look in your eyes when you argue that women should be educated. It's the way your arms tense up when you tell others that we should not be traded as property. It's that smile (it's just nice that you have most of your teeth, honestly). Shall we meet for the protest outside the National Assembly at dawn?

Mary Wollstonecraft

♡

---

* Wollstonecraft was a huge advocate of women's rights, arguing that women were not naturally inferior to men. Maybe that's why she ended up marrying William Godwin, a forefather of the anarchist movement and a true crust punk.

♡

Your mind is a blank slate, my dear girl, but I am here to color it with knowledge. What you need is an older man who can define the self through a continuity of consciousness and also survive the Great Plague. I have done both these things. Now I'm afraid your love is as infectious as a rapidly spreading disease, your smile as contagious as an infected rat flea. Sorry, this plague is really getting to me. If we survive, I'd love to see you again.

John Locke

♡

```
  ※ ⊙                    INSTANT MESSENGER              ⊙ ⊘    ⊗
  ⬚ ※ infobot                                                  ▣
```

Ja :: 13:12:23
pomoc

KantOfficial: hai, u up?
WestphalianDogLuvr: who is this? ur not in my contacts
K: it's kant :) :) :) :)
W: …
K: we were in the same class at königsberg, "fun with monads
101" w/ prof knutzen!
W: i think u hav the wrong person. u prolly mixed me up w/
westieGurl99
K: rly? Hmm … i also wrote the critique of pure reason …? ;)
W: o ya!!! i remember u!! wuts up?
K: nm. was just thinking about judgment. i feel like there are
soooo many different kinds of judgment but ppl just throw the
term around like wutever. 4 example, aesthetic judgment:
IMHO, that is HOT 2 b conflated w/ judgment of taste. but i
dunno. ugh wut do u think??? :D
W: i was about 2 go 2 sleep. it's pretty L8 …
K: right, ha ha sorry! i guess i just wanted to tell u that i
was reflecting upon the notion of aesthetic judgment and i've
determined that **u r beautiful** ha ha ;)
W: o thnx kant!!! that's really sweet :)
K: do u know y tho? it's cuz this judgment of beauty is based
on a feeling of pleasure
W: ok. i get it. do u want to grab a drink this week or some
thing …?
K: but this pleasure is of a distinctive kind. it's
disinterested
W: so ur not interested? i'm rly confused
K: no no, like because my feelings of pleasure are
disinterested, ur beauty is universal!
W: g2g
K: waaait! have i offended u?!! !! :(:(
W: i'm going 2 bed. byez

[WestphalianDogLuvr is offline]

```
  ⬚ ◈ ◉ ◎ ⌕ 📇 ⬚ ⊙ 🖼
```

```
  B  I  U  ■  ⇨                  ※        SEND        ⌄
```

♡

By the time you finish this letter, you will realize that there is no actual conception of the self. There is no "You" and "I." There are, however, a bundle of sensations that we experience: that day we met outside my family home in Berwickshire; the way you cried ever so deeply when you found out I was an atheist; how repulsed you looked after you discovered I had scurvy. I love you, and these moments make us who we are. I may put the "Hume" in humor, but this is no joke.

David Hume

♡

My dearest Frank, I was instantly drawn to you. Not just because my visa was about to expire, but also because you were surprisingly good looking for an American. Objectivism claims that happiness is the moral purpose of life, and I'm quite sure that objectifying you will make me happy. You live by your own efforts. You honor and respect achievement. You stay on your side of the bed. That is all I need.

Ayn Rand

♡

♡

O ÉMILIE DU CHÂTELET, YOU ARE QUITE A DREAM!

I HOPE YOU LIKE CAUSTIC MEN WITH LOW SELF-ESTEEM

THE ONLY THING I'D LOVE MORE THAN SEPARATION OF CHURCH AND STATE

IS TO FINALLY TAKE YOU OUT ON A DATE

THE WAY YOU STUDY PHYSICS MAKES MY HEART GROW WEAK

WHEN YOU TRANSLATE *PRINCIPIA MATHEMATICA*, I CAN BARELY SPEAK

TOGETHER, LET US DETERMINE THE ELEMENTS OF FIRE

AND THEN WHO KNOWS WHAT MAY TRANSPIRE!

THE FRENCH GOVERNMENT CAN TRY TO SUPPRESS MY VIEWS

BUT YOU WILL FOREVER AND ALWAYS BE MY MUSE

ALLOW ME TO LEARN FROM YOUR BRILLIANT MIND

AND OCCASIONALLY GLANCE AT THAT NICE BEHIND.

Voltaire

♡

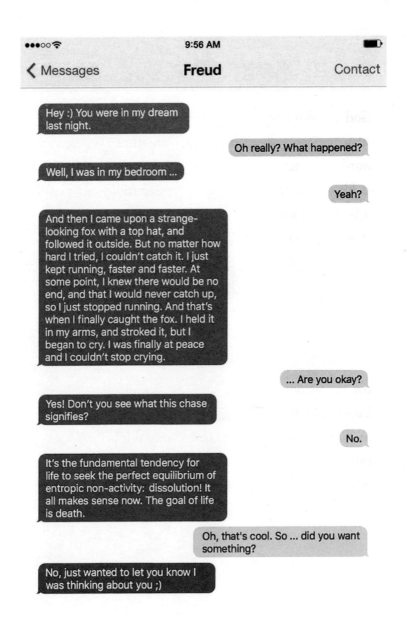

●●●○○ 🛜   9:56 AM   🔋

‹ Messages   **Freud**   Contact

Hey :) You were in my dream last night.

Oh really? What happened?

Well, I was in my bedroom ...

Yeah?

And then I came upon a strange-looking fox with a top hat, and followed it outside. But no matter how hard I tried, I couldn't catch it. I just kept running, faster and faster. At some point, I knew there would be no end, and that I would never catch up, so I just stopped running. And that's when I finally caught the fox. I held it in my arms, and stroked it, but I began to cry. I was finally at peace and I couldn't stop crying.

... Are you okay?

Yes! Don't you see what this chase signifies?

No.

It's the fundamental tendency for life to seek the perfect equilibrium of entropic non-activity: dissolution! It all makes sense now. The goal of life is death.

Oh, that's cool. So ... did you want something?

No, just wanted to let you know I was thinking about you ;)

♡

If God is infinitely good, and Christ links God with His creatures, then you are the finest creature I've ever seen. Edward, if I may be so bold, you appear to be a man who likes a good adventure. If persecution and possible imprisonment intrigues you, I'm converting to Quakerism next week. Join me.

Anne Conway

♡

Allow me to deduce the reason we should be together. If Aristotle is a man, and all men enjoy sexual intercourse, then Aristotle would surely enjoy sexual intercourse. Now I know what you're thinking. You're afraid I'm using you as an instrumental good. But you can't blame me if that end is happiness. Let's just say I'll see you at nine.

Aristotle

♡

♡

We desire meaning, and yet we cannot have it. Instead we are bound to live a tragic existence, trying to make sense of a world in which I am forced to write you *six* letters in a row, and receive no response. Six. Don't you understand? I desire you, and yet I cannot have you. Why does the Absurd taunt me so? Is it something I said? Seriously, you can tell me. I can no longer stand the cruel, indifferent silence of the universe. Like, just a response would be nice. Or you know what? I don't even care anymore. Don't go out with me. I'm going to die soon anyway,* and life is better without meaning. That way I can never be disappointed.

Albert Camus

♡

---

* Camus was convinced that he would die at an early age. He not only carried a suicide note written by Trotsky's friend in his pocket, but also asked his girlfriend to send him copies of *Embalmer Monthly* magazine. His biggest fear was dying before he had time to finish his works, or at least his love letters.

♡

The persona may be a mask for the collective psyche, but I can no longer mask my feelings for you. I wish to learn and understand your true character, unmediated by society. For example, are you the kind of person that expects me to pay on the first date? Do you really want to be in a committed relationship, or is that just what society is *telling* you to want? There is so much to uncover and so little time! Well, what do you say? It will just be me and you ... and several other psychiatrists of course, so we can get more opinions.

Carl Jung

♡

COPENHAGEN, DENMARK
10 OCTOBER, 1840

HELLO REGINA, SOVEREIGN QUEEN OF MY HEART. IF
YOU DON'T KNOW WHAT THIS IS, IT IS A TELEGRAM. IT
WAS JUST INVENTED. DO YOU REMEMBER THE DAY
WE MET? I DO. IT WAS A SPRING DAY. YOU WERE THE
TENDER AGE OF FOURTEEN. I WAS MERELY TWENTY
FOUR YEARS OLD. ANYWAY, I AM SENDING THIS
INCREDIBLE FORM OF TECHNOLOGY TO INQUIRE AS
TO WHETHER YOU WILL BE FREE IN PRECISELY ONE
MONTH FROM NOW. WOULD YOU BE INTERESTED IN
SOME BEER AND TREMBLING? PERHAPS YOU ARE IN
DANGER? IF SO, LET ME BE YOUR KIERKEGAARDIAN
ANGEL. OKAY. SORRY. I'M DONE. HOPE TO SEE YOU
NEXT MONTH.

SØREN KIERKEGAARD

♡

Man is condemned to be free, without any plans for this Saturday night, so allow me to propose an idea. Existence is inexplicable, which is why we should embrace it together— this weekend perhaps? If we eventually interact in a vaguely romantic setting, I assure you, we would only live our most authentic lives. My ideal date is one in which we stray from the expectations of the bourgeois, and I am sure you agree. I know this because I can see you are conscious of death, my dear girl. You are undoubtedly awake! So, Saturday, then?

Jean-Paul Sartre

Dear little being, what an excellent idea! I was sitting here thinking about how the social construction of Woman as the quintessential Other enables oppression when I got your letter, and was so pleased to receive it. Today the rain is terribly heavy and I'm stuck in a café in Urmatt, but I would love to see you again. I get back into Paris on Saturday, and I'll wire you the exact time. Goodbye for now.

Simone de Beauvoir

♡

♡

Let us protest against the sordid state of intellectualism together. Maybe this is the German idealism talking, but I think this relationship could really work! I perceive you to be a sweet and gentle man. I can already tell you're the kind of guy who puts the seat back down without being asked and believes in the inherent goodness of people. I need some real movement that will make me work, and I'm not just talking about Transcendentalism.

Margaret Fuller

♡

It is essential to do unto others as you would have them do unto you. And what I certainly do not wish for myself is another disappointing date. How can we live our fullest, most compassionate lives by just going to the same bars over and over again? This is the time for change. The Golden Age of dating is not over. No, it has just begun.

Confucius

♡

♡

I couldn't help but notice you were reading Wittgenstein's *Tractatus Logico-Philosophicus* the other day outside of class. That's my absolute *favorite* book, after the Bible.* Would you like to grab lunch tomorrow and discuss how consequentialism is morally flawed? I may disagree with Bentham and Mill's utilitarianism, but I can still show you a good time.

Elizabeth Anscombe

♡

I recently got the latest astrolabe, if you'd like to come over and check it out. Now I know why you may be hesitating. Many think I am a witch, but I assure you, it is not so. I just like to know the position of the Sun and Moon at all times, and I believe the stars are telling me we should be positioned closer together.*

Hypatia of Alexandria

---

* Anscombe was probably the world's greatest teacher's pet. She edited and translated several volumes from Wittgenstein's notebooks and was even awarded the Austrian Cross of Honour for all that work. What a champ.

* Being an astronomer in 4th-century Egypt was like being in the Mafia. You were part of an exclusive, influential group, would constantly get into fights and always feared for your life. This was especially true for Hypatia. She loved studying celestial bodies, but was called a Hellenistic pagan and eventually murdered by a Christian mob.

♡

From: martin.heidegger@uni-marburg.de
To: hannah.arendt@uni-marburg.de
Subject: Thinking of you (and the notion of concrete existence)
Date: 20 September, 1925 2:15 PM

Dear Hannah,

I adore you, but know that I cannot have you. You are my student, and to make matters worse, I am a married man. I have been wondering about what it means for something to truly be, but cannot focus when I think about last night. How do I strive for authenticity in human existence if we continue to make out after class, completely undisclosed?

Best,
Martin

Martin Heidegger
Philosophy Professor
University of Marburg
Biegenstraße 10, 35037
Marburg, Germany
O: +49 6421 5304
"Why are there beings at all, instead of Nothing?"—Me

♡

♡

From: hannah.arendt@uni-marburg.de
To: martin.heidegger@uni-marburg.de
Subject: Re: Thinking of you (and the notion of concrete existence)
Date: 20 September, 1925 4:23 PM

Dear Martin,

I feel the same way. I have so much to learn from you. Your teaching methods are unorthodox to be sure, but invaluable nonetheless. Nothing riles you up more than discussing the origins of totalitarianism, and I love that about you. Rather than meeting in the janitor's closet next time, how about we convene in the riverside park near campus and make out there? For our speaking and acting to be authentic forms of expression, I strongly believe we must appear in a public space. Trust me. This way, we'll be free, powerful, and equal—the last of which hopefully gets us over that *banal* student-teacher barrier you keep rambling on about.

Yours,
Hannah

♡

♡

Is it better to be loved than feared or feared than loved? I have always found it safer to be feared, but with you, something feels different. I find myself being able to "trust" again, although can you ever truly "trust" "anyone?" Dishonesty and deviousness are surely useful in the political realm, but I want to be honest with you. Let me begin by confessing that I *was* friends with Leonardo da Vinci, but we never did end up stealing the Arno River like I said.* I'm changing, though, I promise. It is 1505, after all. New Year, New Me!

Niccolò Machiavelli

♡

---

* Strangely enough, Machiavelli and da Vinci passed the time in 16th-century Florence by hatching up crazy schemes together. One of them involved re-routing all the water from the Arno River Valley directly to Florence to get back at their arch-nemesis city, Pisa. The plan was too crazy and never worked out, but it signified one of the earliest Italian bromances.

I'm staring at an old photograph of us, but can't figure it out. We're at a bar and looking off into the distance at something, I can't remember what it was. I do know that it was '56. You're smiling and holding a glass of wine, which is almost empty. Your hand is gently resting on my arm. Normally, I know all the signs. The wine is our signifier, of course, and the signified is a hopeless bourgeois ideal. But ... what did it all *mean*? I thought we were having a nice time. And yet you never called. Why? I thought I could employ semiotics to understand what went wrong, but apparently I have much to learn.

Roland Barthes

♡

The goal of self-dating is to gain a deep knowledge of oneself, of what one really is and wants, so that, by way of taking a vow to my deeper Self, I can achieve self-acceptance and self-harmonization, and this will enable me to lead a deeply satisfied life ... will it? They say that in order to love others, you have to love yourself—truly? What if the opposite holds, at two levels: I love others to escape myself, and I can only love myself insofar as I am able to love others? Self-marrying presupposes that I've found peace with myself—but what if I cannot reconcile myself with myself? And what if I fully discover this only after I got married to myself? Should I enact a formal proceeding of self-divorce? Should this divorce be permitted for Catholics ...?

Slavoj Žižek

♡

♡

From: william.duBois@wilberforce.edu
To: nina.gomer@wilberfoce.edu
Subject: Souls of (Two) Black Folk Should Have Dinner Tonight
Date: 12 October, 1895 3:04 PM

My dear Nina,

You were truly excellent in class the other day, so I thought
I'd shoot you an e-mail. I believe that fully understanding the
identity of double consciousness faced by African Americans
is *so* essential, but I want to make sure you absolutely get it.
Maybe we could go over the intellectual and cultural parity
between black and white cultures over dinner tonight?

Very sincerely yours,
W.E.B. Du Bois

W.E.B. Du Bois
Wilberforce University
1055 N Bickett Rd
Wilberforce, OH 45384
O: (937) 452 - 7654
"The cost of liberty is less than the price of repression."—Me

♡

♡

Look, I'll be honest with you. I'm not a popular man. I'm not a wealthy man. I'm not a funny man. I'm not even a healthy man. I really might be dying—I feel terrible. But I *am* a simple lens grinder with a lot of heart. Of course, the criterion of truth is not sensory but intellectual, and I wish to be rational about all this, but I can't help it. When I grind those optical lenses each day, I look around at all the sparkling glass dust and breathe in deep because it feels like I'm breathing in *magic*. Like we're one step closer to being together. I feel lightheaded! And I know it's either because I'm deeply in love or have tuberculosis.*

Baruch Spinoza

♡

I've loved you ever since we were children. Some of my dearest memories involve playing in the streets of Trier and reading about political liberalism together in secret. Seeing as we're both workers of the world, I was thinking we could unite over a pint of Krombacher later?

Karl Marx

♡

---

* Spinoza enjoyed working as a lens grinder but ended up dying at the age of 44 from a lung illness after inhaling a lot of glass dust. Another explanation is he died from a broken heart, but it's not as likely.

♡

Dear Lou,

Below you will find ten reasons why I believe we should be married*:

1. I know I proposed to you twice before and you refused, but I am positive that third time's the charm.
2. You're the first female psychoanalyst, which I totally respect.
3. You get along well with Freud, so I already know you're great with my friends.
4. You're my favorite intellectual protégé.
5. You love writing about the erotic nature of women and how sexual difference runs deeper than economics. I'm very into that, and also enjoy anything erotic.
6. We're both big Ibsen fans.
7. You always smell nice.
8. I adore your boyish curiosity and rugged complexion.
9. We both share a passion for critiquing reason and rejecting objective truth.
10. I am so alone.

Friedrich Nietzsche

---

* In August 1882, Nietzsche sent his ten stylistic rules of writing in a series of letters to Lou Andreas-Salomé, the first female psychoanalyst. Nietzsche allegedly proposed marriage at their second meeting, and although she rejected him several times, she ended up including his ten rules of writing in a book she wrote on him. Hopefully that makes up for it.

Philosophers' Missed Connections

?

M / 4 / W

Copenhagen, Denmark. Outside the Royal Theatre

You were enjoying a carriage ride last week, and you looked so serene. I wanted to stop the carriage and sit down next to you, but you rode away instead. I wish I had stopped that carriage and said hello. I also would have probably returned home about five hours earlier.

?

P

W / 4 / M
Jena, Germany. University campus

We were both at the protest last week, but you didn't seem to notice me. You were wearing a black cloak, torn at the sleeves, and I was pretending to read Hegel's new book. I thought I saw you look at me, but you might have just been on the lookout for the police. I watched you chain yourself to a fence. I wish with all my heart I were that fence.

P

M / 4 / M
Paris, France, while we were storming the Bastille

Things were pretty hectic, but I noticed you right away. You were carrying a torch and had blood running down the side of your face, yet I could still tell you were cute. If France becomes a democratic nation and we both survive the revolution, we should grab coffee.

P

♀

W / 4 / M
Athens, Greece. By the river
I was washing my clothes, and you walked by with your lamb. You had a long beard, just like everyone else in Athens, but something felt different about yours. I wanted to say hi, but I mostly wanted to kill the lamb. I was very hungry and had not eaten in two days.

♀

M / 4 / M
Lu, Zhou Dynasty. Calligraphy class
You sat across from me in class, and I saw you practicing. Did you notice me too? There is nothing I love more than good penmanship. I want you to hold me the way you hold that bamboo brush, delicate yet firm, with the desire to create something beautiful. If you see this and feel the same way, sit beside me in charioteer class next week.

♀

?

W / 4 / M

London, England. Inside bakery

We were both reaching for the same loaf of bread and our hands touched. I noticed you were reading Henry More's *Platonicall Song of the Soul*, and mentioned that More happened to be my tutor. We laughed and you let me have the loaf of bread. Care to split it with me?

?

M / 4 / W

Zürich, Switzerland. Psychiatric hospital

I was in the hallway discussing the pathology of occult phenomena when you walked by. I could hardly speak and instantly felt faint, but was not sure if that was a result of your beauty or my psychosis. Either way, we should make time for psychoanalysis so that we can get to know one another.

?

Staying in Love

Mix Tapes

*The songs philosophers would
choose for their ultimate mix*

♪

Sigmund Freud

I Love My Momma—Snoop Dogg

The Father Who Must Be Killed—Morrissey

Dreams—Fleetwood Mac

♪

Ayn Rand

Objectivist on Fire—Bayside

Can't Get Enough of Myself—Santigold

Eye of the Tiger—Survivor

♪

♪

Socrates

How Might I Live—Real Estate

Chamber of Reflection—Mac DeMarco

The Execution of All Things—Rilo Kiley

♪

Niccolò Machiavelli

The First Cut is the Deepest—Sheryl Crow

Back Stabbers—the O'Jays

We Used to be Friends—The Dandy Warhols

♪

♪

Martin Heidegger

Sukie in the Graveyard—Belle and Sebastian

Man of Constant Sorrow—Bob Dylan

Don't Stand So Close to Me—The Police

♪

Immanuel Kant

Follow the Rules—Livin' Joy

A Well Respected Man—The Kinks

99 Problems—Jay-Z

♪

♪

Hypatia of Alexandria

The Celibate Life—The Shins

Alone Again (Naturally)—Gilbert O'Sullivan

Like a Virgin—Madonna

♪

Karl Marx

Working Class Hero—John Lennon

I'm a Slave 4 U—Britney Spears

Work—Rihanna

♪

♪

Friedrich Nietzsche

Bored in the USA—Father John Misty

Losing My Religion—R.E.M.

Stronger—Kanye West

♪

Albert Camus

Ready to Die—The Notorious B.I.G.

There is a Light that Never Goes Out—The Smiths

Rebel Rebel—David Bowie

♪

♪

David Hume

Listen to Your Heart—Roxette

Wonderwall—Oasis

Love in this Club—Usher

♪

John Searle

Computer Love—Kraftwerk

Yoshimi Battles the Pink Robots—The Flaming Lips

Paranoid Android—Radiohead

♪

♪

Simone de Beauvoir

Modern Girl—Sleater-Kinney

Bad Reputation—Joan Jett

No Scrubs—TLC

♪

Dear Descartes: Part 1

Philosophers have a lot to say about love with their very own advice columns

Socratic Sexts

Dear Socrates,

I'm dating a philosopher, sort of like you, even though I hear you're being executed soon ... anyway, I still thought you could help while you have some time left. I don't know what to do. He's a great guy, but he only speaks in metaphors, and I honestly never *really* know what he's talking about. The other day he told me he was trapped in a cave, and then escaped. Except where we live, there are a lot of caves. Not sure whether he means a metaphorical cave of ignorance or a literal cave. I am very confused. Please advise.

Sincerely,
Figuratively Frustrated

––––

Dear Figuratively Frustrated,

Sounds like you have a true dilemma on your hands, but don't worry, I'm here to help. Many know me for claiming that the "unexamined life is not worth living," but I also believe that the "unexamined wife is unforgiving." This means that we must always be questioning our partners to find out what is wrong, or face the consequences. Remember, communication is always the key to a healthy relationship, so I suggest using the Socratic method to get to the root of your problems. It's a dialectical approach that is sure to stimulate critical thinking and help you grow closer as a couple. You will definitely argue and hate each other at first, but you'll thank me later.

'Til death,
Socrates

Purely Platonic

Dear Plato,

My wife and I have been married for twenty years now. We met at an execution and have been in love ever since. But lately, things have changed. She flinches when I try to kiss her and she hardly ever wants to sleep with me anymore. Believe me, I have tried everything. Bought her new robes. Found her fresh drinking water. Explained that we must procreate for the good of the community. But nothing seems to be working. What should I do? Is our relationship doomed?

From,
Lacking Love

———

Dear Lacking Love,

You are going about this all wrong. Do not confuse love with carnal desire. I don't know if you've ever read *Symposium* (it was my bestseller), but in this work I discuss how the true goal of erôs is real beauty. Don't you see? Physical contact is wasteful and blinds you from using this love to reach higher pursuits. Take it from me—sex is overrated. Am I still a virgin? Sure. Do I dream of human touch constantly? *Of course.* But that is beside the point.

Best of luck,
Plato

Kant Live Without You

Dear Immanuel,

I am worried that my boyfriend is cheating on me. He comes home late at night, drunk and smelling of cheese, does not wish to speak with me and always looks tired. I know he is working long hours at the cheese factory, but that can't just be it. How do I know for sure if he is being faithful? Should I ask him or search for clues? Desperate for answers and don't know where to begin.

Yours,
Clueless

Dear Clueless,

While you seek these answers, know that you must remain rational. Ask yourself, "What can I know?" and recognize that knowledge only comes from experience. You cannot know for sure that he has cheated on you if you have no evidence. That's what I tell my partner all the time. Now I am sure your boyfriend is innocent, for if he was following the categorical imperative and cheating, then you could theoretically cheat on him as well. Not an ideal situation, but a possible one.

Universal Law is Life,
Immanuel Kant

For a Nietzsche Audience

Dear Friedrich,

I recently got out of a long-term relationship and have been feeling very lost. It's as if I'm not myself anymore and I don't know what to do. Everything reminds me of our time together, like when we stayed in all day and made Mässmogge candies. That was a good day. Will I ever feel normal again?

Yours,
Broken Boy

———

Dear Broken Boy,

You need to get a grip. Mässmogge candies? What are you even talking about? Look, when I realized that God was dead I was pretty upset, too. Couldn't eat, couldn't sleep, all of that nonsense. But then I realized that our existence has no meaning, and I *pulled it together*. I don't adhere to the narrow limits set by God, and you don't need to feel confined by a relationship anymore! It's time to seriously re-evaluate your life. Delete their number, stop following them on social media. This ex should be completely dead to you, because in the end, you only have yourself anyway.

Sincerely,
Friedrich Nietzsche

Simone Says:
Mastering the Game of Love

Dear Simone,

I have been in a serious relationship for three years now, and we have always been very happy, but my boyfriend has been acting different lately. Whenever we are out, I notice him giving out to his number to multiple women, or shouting, "I hate relationships!" at the top of his lungs. I am beginning to sense that he wants to start seeing other people. I could see myself marrying him one day, but maybe he does not feel the same way. Should I confront him about it or just break up with him?

From,
Afraid to Ask

————

Dear Afraid to Ask,

It sounds like he might want to take a break, but you never know. If you feel that he is interested in other women, why not allow yourself to explore as well? Open relationships have always worked wonders for me, but you need to set some ground rules first. What I like to do is have an "essential" lover, and then "contingent" love affairs whenever they are desired. If this works out, you can eventually experiment with an open marriage as well. This way, you can challenge the social construct of marriage while saving your relationship!

Sincerely,
Simone de Beauvoir

Hume Finds You a Groom

Dear David,

I am utterly heartbroken. Recently, I've fallen in love with someone, but I know it will never work out. We flirt all the time, yet she is a married woman, and would never want to hurt her family. I understand that, but I still can't stop thinking about her. When we talk and text it feels so unethical, yet I still want us to be together one day. Does this make me a bad person?

Hopelessly,
Lost in Love

――――

Dear Lost in Love,

You are going about this all wrong! This reminds me of that time I told a buddy of mine, "Reason is, and ought to be the slave of the passions." I even made it my Twitter bio for a while. Well, I still stand by that today. Ethics should be based on real emotion, not some abstract moral principle. If you really love this woman, go get her, tiger!

Sincerely,
David Hume

Love Voltaire Us Apart

Dear Voltaire,

I would lose my head if anyone knew I was writing to you, but my thoughts haunt me, and I decided I had to ask. I am a priest and both my body and spirit belong to the Catholic Church. I love practicing celibacy. It's what I signed on for. I get it. But sometimes ... my mind begins to wander. Why do you choose this life of hedonism? What is it like? Help me understand.

Sincerely,
Puzzled Priest

————

Dear Puzzled Priest,

Oh father, forgive me, for I have *sinned!* Let me tell you, being banned from multiple cities really makes you realize what you want. For there is nothing quite like reading a salacious poem from start to finish. Or caressing a woman until you feel truly enlightened. Otherwise, what's the point?

Gros Bisous,
Voltaire

QUIZ: Getting (Meta)Physical– Who is Your Philosopher Crush?

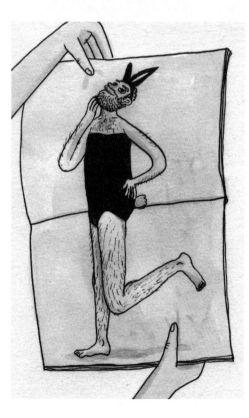

Does the Socratic method make your heart tick?
Should you finally lock it down with John Locke?
Take this quiz to find out!

1. Your ideal first date is:

A Reading philosophy together.

B Attending a university lecture.

C Talking about deep-seated issues you have with your father.

D Going to see live music.

2. Your crush's favorite food is:

A Freshly hunted pheasant.

B Retribution, served cold.

C Homemade apfelstrudel.

D Anything they can find in the dumpster.

3. Your ideal vacation would be:

A Establishing the first library in the ancient Macedonian city of Stagira.

B Staying at home. Vacations are for the weak.

C Exploring the unconscious.

D Escaping the Franco-Prussian War.

4. The most important quality in a partner is:

A Passion. If he doesn't flee his home for his beliefs, he's not for you.

B Moral duty. You like when he sticks to his convictions, even if it alienates everyone around him.

C Creativity. You need someone who loves to dream, and then analyze those dreams as wish-fulfillments.

D Confidence. Übermensch doesn't even begin to cover it.

5. The most important thing in life is:

A Understanding the connection between beauty and truth.

B Proving that reason is the source of morality.

C Analyzing your repressed desires.

D Death.

6. The people you date are usually:

A Understanding and intelligent.

B Cautious and dramatic.

C Neurotic and troubled.

D Overly critical and misunderstood.

7. If you could switch jobs, your next profession would be:

A A tutor.

B A professor.

C A psychoanalyst.

D All and none of the above.

8. What best describes your sense of style?

A Warm and comfortable. Nothing's better than a homespun cloak and a tunic.

B Classy and elegant. Give me a formal robe and a petticoat, and I'm good to go on a morning stroll.

C Quirky and reeking of cigar smoke. I love wearing bright dirndls that match my apron.

D Anything that is black. Is this over yet?

9. You broke up with your last partner because:

A He didn't believe that knowledge came from sensory experience.

B He wasn't serious enough.

C He wanted to sleep with his mother.

D I didn't. He died from smallpox.

10. When it comes to looks, your ideal mate is:

A Skinny and slightly nerdy.

B Well dressed, with a cute wig.

C Grizzly, and maybe a bit plump—more to love!

D Tall, dark, and some weird facial hair.

If you chose mostly As, you should date:

ARISTOTLE

You want someone who will help you question and understand your moral obligations. Aristotle is reserved and level-headed, but also intense. He cares about ethical behavior more than anything, and that's a huge turn on! Just be willing to let him go if he has to suddenly flee the city for his beliefs.

If you chose mostly Bs, you should date:

IMMANUEL KANT

What a keeper! Kant can be pretty strict sometimes, but he also knows how to let loose and make you feel alive when it counts. As hard as you try, you never really feel like you understand him, but you like the mystery. It's imperative that you don't let this one go.

If you chose mostly Cs, you should date:

SIGMUND FREUD

Remember to watch out! Sigmund really knows how to get inside your head, so you've got to be careful. Sure, he has a lot of unhealthy erotic attachments and an overactive libido, but you like the challenge. The only thing this bad boy is repressing is a lot of neurotic guilt, and his love for you!

If you chose mostly Ds, you should date:

FRIEDRICH NIETZSCHE

God may be dead, but your love life sure isn't! Nietzsche is the kind of guy you can cuddle with on those rainy, cold days, even if afterwards you will probably still feel empty inside. He can be a bit of a downer sometimes, but you find his pessimism adorable and endearing.

Dear Descartes: Part II

Arendt You Happy To See Me?

Dear Hannah,

I just started seeing someone and I'm definitely enjoying our time together, but we don't have much in common and I always thought I'd date someone who shared more of my interests. Sometimes I even think she might be annoyed that I'm vegan. I didn't think these small things would matter to me, but now I'm not sure. How do I know if I should stick it out?

From,
Conflicted

————

Dear Conflicted,

I don't understand the problem. You say you love this person, so I don't see why anything else matters. What, your partner likes *Girls* but you're a *Broad City* fan? Big deal. Heidegger is affiliated with the Nazis and I am a Jew in 1930s Germany. The Gestapo arrested me and yet it changes nothing! Heidegger still writes to me, that fool. But when we critique the metaphysical tradition's move toward abstract contemplation, I remember why I love him. If you really care about this person, you'll be able to move past any minor differences.

Yours,
Hannah Arendt

2 Fast 2 Confucius

Dear Confucius,

My partner's birthday is coming up and I want to do something really special. Usually, we just go to Benihana and order a lot of extra shrimp. It is awesome. But I feel like this year I should be more romantic and maybe even throw a surprise party. I know surprise parties are usually the worst, but maybe this one will be fun? Hope this is the right way to go.

Yours,
Out of Ideas

————

Dear Out of Ideas,

If you do not like surprise parties, why throw one? One of my most well-known principles states, "Do unto others as you would have them do unto you." This holds true even here. There's nothing wrong with trying something new, but you should act with kindness, and everyone knows nothing good will come of a surprise party. Just stick with Benihana. You can't go wrong with the shrimp.

Best,
Confucius

Love Lock(e)down

Dear John,

I am leaving for college in the Fall, but I'm still a virgin and afraid I don't have enough experience. I don't even know where to buy my own khakis. What if I say something stupid? Where do I put my hands? I have so many questions and didn't know where else to go. I know we've never met, but you're sort of the closest thing I ever had to a dad, so please, be honest: am I doomed?

From,
Inexperienced

____

Dear Inexperienced,

First, I want to say I'm flattered you consider me a father figure. Second, do not worry! At birth, the mind is a blank slate and you're meant to experience these things in time! Go skinny-dipping! Take some challenging, yet rewarding introductory philosophy classes! Get your first STD and then email your mom asking for help! This is the only way you can ever define the self.

Sincerely,
John Locke

X Marx the Spot

Dear Karl,

There's this girl I know. She's my best friend but I'm in love with her. I already told her how I feel and I think it's going really well … except for the fact that we've never kissed. She always has me buy her stuff, but she then only goes on dates with other people. I know she's definitely into me, but what else could I be doing to really revolutionize the progress of this relationship?

Yours,
Fool in Love

––––

Dear Fool in Love,

I could not have chosen a better name for you. Fool, indeed! This situation is what Engels would call a classic case of "false consciousness." You think you're getting closer to something real and tangible, but you couldn't be further away. In fact, you are being blatantly exploited, and suffering dearly. Material processes, such as this "stuff" you claim to buy her, simply mask your true relations. You have clearly been friend-zoned and can't even see it. Free yourself before it's too late.

Sincerely,
Karl Marx

Take My Rand in Marriage (Or Not, Who Cares)

Dear Ayn,

I've been single for a few years now, and I'm fine with it. I'm happy being on my own. I know who I am. But sometimes I wonder if I'll ever find someone. I feel like I'm almost destined to be single and that scares me a little. I know I should stop worrying, but I can't help it. What would you do?

Yours,
Single and Sulking

——

Dear Single and Sulking,

Let me tell you a story about someone who came from Russia to the United States in 1926. This person had nothing, only the view of the Manhattan skyline, but it was enough. Thirty years later, this person became incredibly famous and was known as the most creative thinker alive. No, I am not talking about Kanye West. This person I am talking about is myself. You can be just as successful as I am if you never let a man get in your way. Remember, "To say 'I love you' one must first be able to say the 'I.'"

Sincerely,
Ayn Rand

The Original Prince Charming

Dear Niccolò,

I just remarried and have already run into some problems. She has kids from a previous marriage and they don't seem to like me very much. How can I make them feel more comfortable around me?

From,
Remarried

____

Dear Remarried,

Let me tell you exactly what you must do. You are the "new prince" of the family, so to speak. Now is the time to stabilize your power before it is too late. Do not be above brute force or deceit to get what you desire. If they don't get up for school in time, turn back the clocks. Teach them a lesson they'll never forget. They may not be happy at first, but if they end up respecting you, the ends will justify the means. Remember, mercy is weakness.

Best,
Niccolò Machiavelli

You'll be Søren
the Morning

Dear Søren,

Today I realized I have never been single. I just keep jumping from relationship to relationship, and sometimes I'm worried that I'm afraid to be alone. I don't know what I want exactly, but I think I need to find out. Is breaking up the only way?

Yours,
Never Been Single

____

Dear Never Been Single,

I believe it was Beyoncé who was once up in the club after a breakup, just doing her own little thing. However, she is only able to do her own little thing because she realized that truth is subjective. You must learn to embrace being a single lady, and more importantly, a single individual. This is the only way to prioritize concrete human reality over abstract thinking.

Sincerely,
Søren Kierkegaard

How to Know if Your Man is Writing a Manifesto

We've all been there. Maybe you met him at a protest or heard him shout the words "Workers of the world, unite!" And that's when you knew you were hooked. In that moment, you had nothing to lose but your chains (and all your clothes). But maybe he's been acting different lately, or he seems more distant. If you think that it's because he's writing a manifesto, identify the signs before it's too late.

He's always busy

You used to attend lectures at the nearby university together all the time, but now he never wants to leave his apartment. He missed all your friends' birthday parties and even though he told you he "wished he didn't have to read another book about the abysmal state of the economy," you don't believe him.

He's emotionally unavailable

Whenever you tell him that you love him, he responds by reminding you that the inevitable victory of the proletariat is the greatest love of all. You brush the comment aside yet can't help but admit to yourself that it still hurts.

He was expelled from his country

You hardly ever see him anymore because he had to renounce his citizenship, but you want to believe he still cares about you. Now that you're alone, you think about the good old times and wonder if you'll ever see him again.

He formed a secret league

You found him, but you're always surrounded by other people. While you're planning your wedding, he seems to be busy planning imminent revolution with his secret league.

He was banished ... again

Just when you thought you were starting to make the relationship work, isolated riots lead to popular revolt and the government banishes him a second time. It remains doubtful that you'll ever see him again.

~~~

There you have it! If any of these signs seem familiar, then he is probably writing a manifesto. My advice: better to break up now before he makes you proofread any of it.

Breaking Up

US NOT DATING:

LONG-TERM MONOGOMY AND WHY IT'S NOT REALLY WORKING OUT BETWEEN YOU AND ME, SPECIFICALLY

So, You Used to Date a Philosopher

How to get over the breakup

Get plenty of exercise

Try going for a run to get those endorphins pumping. This is the new you, so forget those painful memories and focus on moving forward. Maybe try out the treadmill and see if you feel better, but remember that it is ultimately futile. The treadmill is a metaphor for life—meaningless, cyclical, tiring. You can keep running as fast as you can, but let's face it, Heidegger was right, we cannot live until we face our own mortality.

Cook often and eat healthy!

Your body needs excellent nutrition to function properly. After this breakup, give yourself time to heal and spend your evening making an incredible home-cooked meal for yourself. Sure, you could make a glazed salmon or something, but if you're like me and believe that Plato was correct when he wrote that unchanging reality is the object of knowledge, then you know that some piece of salmon won't truly improve your life. I like to just get a can of split pea soup, throw it in the microwave, and call it a day. Sometimes I feel like the minor explosion that results makes up for the "spark" my so-called relationship never had.

Go on a trip

Vacations are the best way to clear your head and move on. It will also ensure that you don't accidentally run into your ex. Try going to a place with a beach and lots of sun, so you can soak up the rays and come back with a killer tan. However, a cheaper and more rewarding way to escape is by imagining an alternative reality. Nietzsche believed there were no facts, only interpretations. So, why not clear your mind and finally challenge yourself by applying your new perspective to the morally corrupt world around you?

Take up a hobby

There's a chance you have tons of free time now and need to channel all that energy into something positive. John Stuart Mill and Jeremy Bentham would recommend something with a little more utility, seeing as the purpose of morality is to make life better by increasing the amount of pleasure and happiness in the world. Want to start a podcast even though it'll annoy your friends? Do it anyway! Always thought about being a DJ but worried that you'll become an asshole? If it makes you happy, go ahead! Your new, hedonistic lifestyle is only a DJ set away.

Find a rebound

At the end of the day, many an adage recommends that the best way to get over your ex is to get under someone else. Get dressed up, go out, and have sex with *anyone* you can so that your painful memories will slowly fade away. However, you can also try to ease your own suffering by *resisting* sleeping with a complete stranger. After all, as Kant's categorical imperative clearly states, it is immoral to use another person solely as a means to an end. But hey, do whatever you want. I mean, what do I know? I'm just writing this so that Nietzsche might see it and take me back.

Breakup Letters

Philosophers may free your mind,
but they also break your heart

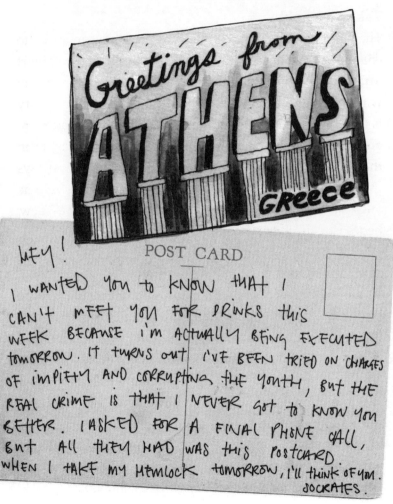

Greetings from ATHENS
GREECE

POST CARD

HEY!

I WANTED YOU to KNOW THAT I
CAN'T MEET YOU FOR DRINKS this
WEEK BECAUSE i'm ACTUALLY BEING EXECUTED
tomorrow. It TURNS OUT I'VE BEEN TRIED ON CHARGES
OF IMPIETY AND CORRUPTING THE YOUTH, BUT THE
REAL CRIME IS THAT I NEVER GOT TO KNOW YOU
BETTER. I ASKED FOR A FINAL PHONE CALL,
BUT ALL THEY HAD WAS THIS POSTCARD.
WHEN I TAKE MY HEMLOCK TOMORROW, I'LL THINK OF YOU
SOCRATES.

It pains me to admit it but Socrates was right about you. You are incapable of thinking about anyone but yourself. When was the last time you even came to see me lecture at the Academy? I have been lost in a state of denial for long enough. Now I finally realize that your love is not true. Your beauty is transcendent, yes, but painfully abstract. Leave me to grapple with the material world. Be gone.

Plato

♥

What are we even doing anymore? With every passing day, you grow more isolated from your labor. We have not made love in over a month, even after I was cured of that rash, and was so certain that we would celebrate appropriately. I demand justice from this bourgeois hand-job hell they call "relationships."

Karl Marx

♥

Do you remember that day with the ducks? It was cold and rainy and the foreboding sky tried to seal our fate with each gust of wind. We hurried underneath the nearest awning, where we came upon a family of ducks nestled together, and I remember looking at you and thinking, "This can't last long." But what ever does? Listen to me when I say that just as a bee abandons its flower once pollination is complete, you too must move onward, or go under. One day soon you will meet a man, and he will rise like a phoenix from the ashes, and it is my greatest hope that he will not give you syphilis.

Friedrich Nietzsche

♥

♡

```
☀ ⊙                    INSTANT MESSENGER          ⌄ ⌃    ⊗
💬 ☀ infobot                                              ▣

Ja :: 13:12:23
pomoc

 KantOfficial: Hey, we need to talk. I know that you're
 online and if you do not wish to answer that's fine, but
 here I go. For our entire relationship I was absolutely
 and irrevocably miserable. I can see now that you used
 me purely as a means to an end. Don't you know how that
 makes me feel? It is imperative that you reflect on the
 meaning of universal law, and stop doing that thing you
 did with your tongue. I hated that.


 [KantOfficial is offline]
```

♡

I drink, therefore I am ... drunk. Ha ha! I thought this would be easier after my sixth glass of wine, but alas, it is still absolutely terrible. Oh, how my world grows smaller when I think of you not in it, and—no, you know what? Let me start over. Philosophy is like a tree, and it has all these branches that extend outward, but you're like a shrub. Cute and small, but not well versed in rationalist thought. Do you get what I'm trying to say?

René Descartes

♡

My dear little girl, I visited the Balzac exhibit the other day and immediately knew what had to be done. I am terribly in love with you, and yet I despise you. Try to understand: I think of you in those small, delicate moments, like when a squirrel hurries across the allée or a homeless man pleasures himself in the bushes of les Tuileries. It might be time that you find someone else who shares your interest in morally evolved threesomes.

Jean-Paul Sartre

♡

J.P., you are an ass.

Simone de Beauvoir

♡

COPENHAGEN, DENMARK
II AUGUST, I84I

MY DEAR REGINA, I WILL PROCEED TO BREAK DOWN OUR
RELATIONSHIP INTO THREE STAGES. OUR FIRST STAGE
IS DEFINED BY AESTHETICS. I WALKED DOWN ONE OF MY
FAVORITE CROOKED STREETS IN COPENHAGEN, WATCHED
YOU STEP OUT OF A CARRIAGE AND KNEW I MUST HAVE YOU.
THE SECOND STAGE OF OUR RELATIONSHIP IS AN ETHICAL
ONE. WHILE I DESIRED TO LAY MY EYES ON YOUR HIDDEN
FLESH, I RECOGNIZED THAT YOU HAD RECENTLY REVEALED
YOUR BODY AND SOUL TO MY GOOD FRIEND HANS, AND KNEW
HE WOULD BE PISSED IF I TRIED ANYTHING. OUR THIRD AND
FINAL STAGE IS RELIGIOUS. I DID NOT CARE MUCH FOR HANS,
SO I SEDUCED YOU. HOWEVER, WE HAVE BOTH COMMITTED A
TREMENDOUS SIN AND THUS WE MUST END THIS IMMORAL
THOUGH TITILLATING TRYST IMMEDIATELY. GOD BLESS.

SØREN KIERKEGAARD

♡

Darling Mainframe,

As you know, we have had a deep love affair that has gone on now for literally years. Before I met you, I admit I used to fool around with a lot of desktops and laptops, but you are something completely different. I also did mess around a long time ago with a Vax 750, and then there was that horrible love affair with a beautiful neural network. Oh, did she put on a good act! But all of those systems are now forgotten. What I love most about you is that you passed all of Alan's tests. Who could worry about syntax and semantics when our relationship was so poetic? But what really broke my heart, I must confess, was when I discovered that you don't really understand Chinese.*

John Searle

♡

* Searle's "Chinese room" argument refuted the claim that it was possible for a computer running a program to have a "mind" and "consciousness" in the same way that people do, which was a shame because he really needed a prom date.

The *Tribune* just made me their first female correspondent and they want to send me to Europe to cover the revolutions in Italy.* I decided I'm going to take the job, because long-distance relationships never work anyway, and there's nothing I love more than pizza and political unrest. Take care of yourself.

Margaret Fuller

* Fuller was the first editor of the transcendentalist journal *The Dial*, and the first woman allowed to use the library at Harvard. In 1846, she was sent to Europe as a correspondent and allied herself with Giuseppe Mazzini, who spearheaded the Italian revolutionary movement. It was sort of like *Eat, Pray, Love*, but with more revolts and executions.

♥

O ÉMILIE DU CHÂTELET, WHAT A TIME IT HAS BEEN!

BUT WE DO HAVE A PROBLEM, MUCH TO MY CHAGRIN

TIME PASSES BY, AND THE DAYS GROW DARK

WE USED TO STUDY FIRE, NOW THERE IS NO SPARK

YOU TOOK ME IN WHEN I FLED TO LORRAINE

KNOW THAT LIVING IN EXILE WITH YOU KEPT ME SANE

BUT NOW THE TIMES HAVE TRULY CHANGED

AS IT SEEMS WE HAVE BECOME ESTRANGED

MY MARQUISE DU CHÂTELET, KNOW THAT IT'S ME, NOT YOU

BUT AFTER ALL THIS TIME, I'M AFRAID WE'RE THROUGH

SURE, WE HAD SIXTEEN WONDERFUL YEARS

AND SO WE MUST REJOICE, PLEASE SHED NO TEARS

YET I'M AFRAID THAT THIS RELATIONSHIP MUST CEASE

FOR I REGRET TO INFORM YOU, I'VE FALLEN IN LOVE WITH MY NIECE.

Voltaire

♥

From: martin.heidegger@uni-marburg.de
To: hannah.arendt@uni-marburg.de
Subject: Need some Being and Time alone
Date: 15 April, 1926 11:20 PM

Dear Hannah,

I visited my favorite graveyard the other day,* and after staring into the depths of Nothing realized I've never felt more alive! That's when I knew that it was time to break up. Surrounded by death, I saw that I had forgotten how to be free and live for myself. Trust me, this is for the best. We can finally strive for true authenticity by seeing other people. I'd say that we should keep in touch and remain friends, but there's no need, as all Being is connected anyway!

Best,
Martin

P.S. Don't worry—I'll still give you a good grade on your final paper.

Martin Heidegger
Philosophy Professor
University of Marburg
Biegenstraße 10, 35037
Marburg, Germany
O: +49 6421 5304
"Every man is born as many men and dies as a single one"—Me

♡

From: hannah.arendt@uni-marburg.de
To: martin.heidegger@uni-marburg.de
Subject: Re: Need some Being and Time alone
Date: 16 April, 1926 2:04 AM

Martin,

How could you do this? I was your best student. I stayed with you even after we made love that time and you silently lay in bed, correcting my papers. I trimmed your mustache ... twice. Was it *inauthentic* when we visited my childhood home in Berlin and you met my parents? You'll probably find another student to admire you. But you will always feel empty inside. You're a cruel man, Martin, and you don't know the first thing about living.

-H

Sent from my iPhone

♡

---

* When Heidegger was asked how we could recover authenticity, he said that we should try to "spend more time in graveyards." He also probably thought it made a quirky, yet affordable date spot.

♥

There are crimes of passion and crimes of logic, but I'm afraid I am guilty of both. If one is disenchanted with the contemporary system, it is his duty to rebel. In this case, I have rebelled against the sordid institution of marriage by cheating on you multiple times with María Casares (you might have met before, she's the lead actress in my latest play). While I seek justice by opposing this marriage, I still value every human life and will never forget about you. I hope to see you at my next show, and please bring the kids!

Albert Camus

♥

I'm not sure how to tell you this, but we can never see each other again. I know you probably think this is coming out of nowhere, but I have a good reason. It's not you, *or* me— it's the entire Jewish community.* They read some of my writing and decided to expel me from the congregation. It's been great getting to know you, but it's probably best if we ended all communication since I'll be going off the grid for a while. I hope you find another Jewish man to make you happy.

Baruch Spinoza

---

* Spinoza was shunned from the congregation of Amsterdam when he was 23 because his writing was deemed too controversial. He spent his remaining 21 years preaching tolerance and benevolence, and probably talking to his therapist about getting excommunicated.

♡

I know you want us to be "in love" and to "care for one another." But when you try to define what we are and give me the label of "boyfriend," you allow us to become consumable objects, and in turn, mindless consumers. I will not be a slave to the capitalist market or some pathetic Valentine's Day scam. How's this for a Hallmark card? Roses are red. Violets are blue. The author is dead, and so is this relationship.

Roland Barthes

♡

What else is there to say? I just need some time alone. My Objectivist movement is really starting to take off and we got a great new office, so I can't be wasting any time focusing on *men* or *relationships* or *feelings*. Let's be rational about this. I'm not sure how I feel about you, so it's probably best to end things now before I invest any more time. I'm sure you understand!

Ayn Rand

♡

I was told we could only use carrier pigeons for medical emergencies, but this is an emergency of the heart. I've been having strange dreams lately and finally had Freud interpret them. He said they indicate the failure of a marriage for money, which is probably because you're the second-richest heiress in Switzerland. Now I think he might be on to something, and seeing as I've been falling in love with one of my patients, it might be best to go on a short break. If you love something, you have to let it go, sort of like this pigeon. I *do* really need the pigeon back, though, so if you could let it go, that'd be great.

Carl Jung

♡

We clearly tried to make this work, but we can't keep fooling ourselves. Although I remain celibate, and sometimes wonder what a physical relationship might be like, my unwavering affection for mathematics and philosophy is all I need. How can I devote myself to another person when I am already committed to learning everything there is to know about Christianity and the natural world? It's been fun, but I have a lecture I need to prepare for and really should be going.

Hypatia of Alexandria

♡

I know I haven't been around much lately, and I'm sorry. We just opened the Lyceum, and it's doing really well, but needs a lot of work. An intern ordered the wrong tiles the other day, so *that's* a complete disaster. But I don't want to talk about work again. I want to talk about us, because I realized it's unethical to stay together. I'm always talking about how important it is to develop virtues of character and do the right thing. Well, a virtuous man is brave, so here I go—I feel suffocated. I want to see other people. I'm embarrassed when you come by the Lyceum to visit me. I just want it all to end. Man, that actually felt pretty good.

Aristotle

♡

I have been jailed and tirelessly tortured these past few months, yet it is nothing compared to the pain you put me through. Sitting here in my cell has given me a lot of time to reflect and I know this: I do not regret attempting to organize a militia against the return of the Medici family, but I *do* regret walking in on you and my best friend. I regret ever meeting you and only wish we were still together so that you could rot away in here with me.

Niccolò Machiavelli

♡

It turns out you can't handle adventure after all. It shames me to say this, but I cannot believe you are even considered God's creation. Would one of God's creatures stand me up at the theatre, where I was forced to run into my ex and his new lover? I sincerely hope not. You would do well to profoundly reconsider your life choices.

Anne Conway

♡

I'll be honest—I don't have much time left. I can hardly leave my bed and almost suffered another mental breakdown, which my doctor diagnosed as the "Disease of the Learned." But now my gift has gone too far, as everything infuriates me. I can no longer sit idly by as we watch reruns of *Dawson's Creek* and ignore the numerous plot holes. I cannot pretend to laugh at your simple-minded jokes. Respect my dying wish and allow me to suffer in solitude.*

David Hume

♡

---

* Hume attended the University of Edinburgh when he was twelve and while he insisted that there was nothing to learn from his professors, he never graduated. At 25, he had "no source of income and no learned profession," illustrating what it was like to be a 20-something writer in the 18th century.

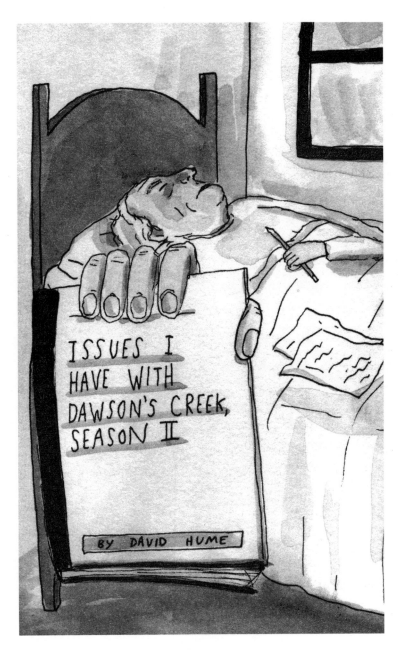

♡

I went to my first feminist zinefest last week and it got me thinking about the patriarchal institution of marriage and its effects on women. Then I thought about our relationship and I made a zine to show you how I feel. Inside you'll find a list of demands for the modern 18th-century woman and a short story about a wife imprisoned in an insane asylum by her husband. I hope you understand that it's probably best if we part ways. And don't worry about keeping the zine, I already made a bunch of copies and started selling them on Etsy.

Mary Wollstonecraft

♡

I'm afraid we don't share the same values. My philosophy emphasizes sincerity and morality, but you're a comedian. I care about ancestral veneration and all you care about is going viral. I'm focused on self-cultivation and you're focused on taking the perfect selfie. We should definitely stop seeing each other, but maybe we'll meet again in the afterlife.

Confucius

♡

Say goodbye to my John Cocke!

John Locke

If Philosophers Starred in Romantic Comedies

Pretty Woman

A Hollywood prostitute, Vivian Ward (Julia Roberts), runs into Karl Marx. He is lost and asks for directions, but Vivian's best friend encourages her to recruit him as a client. It turns out, however, that Marx is completely destitute. Since Marx cannot afford to pay for sex, Vivian suggests they watch *I Love Lucy* reruns instead, but he refuses, reminding her that popular culture is just another way for the dominant class to maintain political and economic power. Vivian cannot afford to go shopping on Rodeo Drive like she imagined, but Marx comforts her by explaining how excessive consumerism only enables commodity fetishism. They live in squalor together, and Vivian remains a prostitute so that they can pay the bills.

How to Lose a Guy in Ten Days

Andie Anderson (Kate Hudson) works for *Composure* magazine, and is writing an article called "How to Lose a Guy in 10 Days" to drive a guy away using classic mistakes women make. At the same time, philosopher Immanuel Kant makes a bet with his friends that he can find happiness and fulfillment in life without using someone as a means to an end. Andie and Kant meet in a bar one night and grow close, but when Kant eventually finds out about the article, he is destroyed. He hurries home and, inspired by his pain, writes *Grounding for the Metaphysics of Morals*, introducing the categorical imperative so that he will never feel hurt again. When Andie hears about Kant's bet, she is pretty confused and still writes her article. They stop speaking after that.

Sleepless in Seattle

After losing his wife to the plague, John Locke tries to start anew in Seattle with his son, Jonah. His son calls in to a radio show and gets Locke to go on air to discuss his wife. Annie Reed (Meg Ryan) is touched, so she writes to John Locke, but his son senses that Annie has absolutely no grasp of epistemology or social contract theory. She just keeps mentioning the Baltimore Orioles, but Jonah knows that his father hates sports. He throws Annie's letters away so that Locke can focus on work instead. Locke's writing ends up influencing the Declaration of Independence, but he dies alone.

The Wedding Singer

Jean-Paul Sartre is an entertaining wedding singer from Ridgefield, New Jersey. He is engaged to his long-time girlfriend, Linda, who was attracted to Sartre at a time when he still dreamed of becoming a rock star. Sartre has also befriended Simone de Beauvoir, a waitress at the reception hall where he usually performs, and Sartre promises to sing at her wedding. After Linda leaves Sartre on their wedding day, Sartre and Simone begin to have feelings for each other. He tries to stop her wedding, but Simone suggests that they just have an open marriage so that she can still hook up with her fiancé, Glenn, on the side. They all live together in New Jersey.

500 Days of Summer

One day, Summer Finn (Zooey Deschanel) meets Friedrich Nietzsche in an elevator. They get along instantly when Summer realizes he is listening to Robert Schumann's Symphony No. 3 in E-flat major. She is also a big fan of Schumann, and sparks fly. They both work at a greeting card company, but Nietzsche is eventually fired when his cards are deemed too dark and not sufficiently "on brand." Summer and Nietzsche call off their relationship when they disagree over the ending of *The Graduate* and the notion of eternal recurrence.

10 Things I Hate About You

A new student at Padua High School, Cameron James, pays Patrick Verona (Heath Ledger) to date the shrewish Ayn Rand so that he can date her sister, Bianca. Patrick and Ayn do not get along right away. Patrick is a bad boy with a temper. Ayn is a libertarian with a heavy Russian accent. But the two eventually get along until Ayn finds out about the arrangement and is heartbroken. For Ayn's final class assignment, instead of sharing her own version of Shakespeare's Sonnet 141, she reads her first draft of *The Fountainhead* from beginning to end. Multiple people ask her to stop, but she keeps going. Patrick keeps the money he won and spends it on more hair gel and black T-shirts.

Annie Hall

Sigmund Freud, a nervous Jewish man, tries to understand why his relationship with Annie (Diane Keaton) ended a year ago. He recalls contemplating the emptiness of existence as a child, and feeling curious about sex at an early age. His relationship eventually falls apart when he buys Annie books on death and suggests she see a psychoanalyst, making her feel inadequate and ultimately pushing her away. It turns out that the film would not change at all.

Glossary

Absolutism

What you *think* it means: The position that in a particular domain of thought, all statements are either absolutely true or absolutely false. These statements are called absolute truths.

What it *really* means: The position that in a particular, long-term relationship or marriage, anything the partner says, no matter how "ridiculous", is absolutely true. These statements are called absolute truths, because otherwise they would be absolutely alone.

Capitalism

What you *think* it means: An economic system in which all or most of the means of production are privately owned, and in which the investment of capital and the production, distribution, and prices of commodities and services are determined mainly in a free market.

What it *really* means: An economic system that thrives upon someone in a relationship fucking up and buying their partner an abundance of unnecessary material gifts to make up for it.

Communism

What you *think* it means: A system of social organization and a political movement based on common ownership of the means of production.

What it *really* means: A polygamous marriage that failed.

Deconstructionism

What you *think* it means: A school and set of methods of textual criticism aimed at understanding the assumptions and ideas that form the basis for thought and belief.

What it *really* means: A school and set of methods aimed at trying to decode late night texts, and understanding why he never called when he said he would.

Defeatism

What you *think* it means: Acceptance of, perhaps even satisfaction with, defeat—taken entirely without struggle.

What it *really* means: Finally letting your parents set you up on a date.

Dualism

What you *think* it means: A set of beliefs with the claim that the mental and the physical are essentially different.

What it *really* means: Accepting that both your mind and body have a fundamentally different nature, and then ignoring both of them after running into your crush and drinking profusely.

Emanationism

What you *think* it means: The belief that reality proceeds from a first principle.

What it *really* means: The belief that reality proceeds from the moment he texts you back after ghosting for a week.

Fatalism

What you *think* it means: The view that human deliberation and actions are pointless and ineffectual in determining events, because whatever will be will be.

What it *really* means: Believing that all human deliberation and actions are pointless while stalking your ex's Facebook photos.

Hedonism

What you *think* it means: The ethical view that pleasure is the greatest good, and that pleasure should be the standard in deciding which course of action to pursue.

What it *really* means: Not feeling guilty on your walk of shame.

Incompatibilism

What you *think* it means: The belief that free will and determinism are not logically compatible categories.

What it *really* means: The belief that a Planned Parenthood director and a Republican on a date are not logically compatible categories.

Mysticism

What you *think* it means: Achieving communion, identity with, or conscious awareness of ultimate reality, the divinity, spiritual truth, or God through direct experience, intuition, or insight.

What it *really* means: Achieving conscious awareness of ultimate reality by meeting the love of your life on the subway.

Nihilism

What you *think* it means: The philosophical view that the world, and especially human existence, is without meaning, purpose, comprehensible truth, or essential value.

What it *really* means: Knowing that human existence is without meaning and purpose after going on your first Tinder date.

A Timeline of Failed Relationships

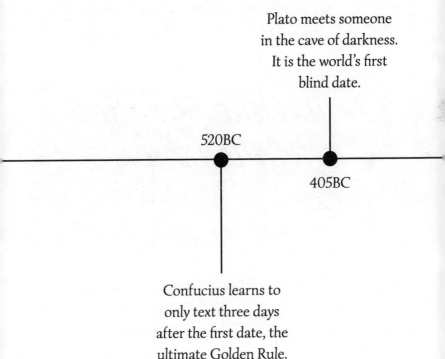

Plato meets someone
in the cave of darkness.
It is the world's first
blind date.

520BC

405BC

Confucius learns to
only text three days
after the first date, the
ultimate Golden Rule.

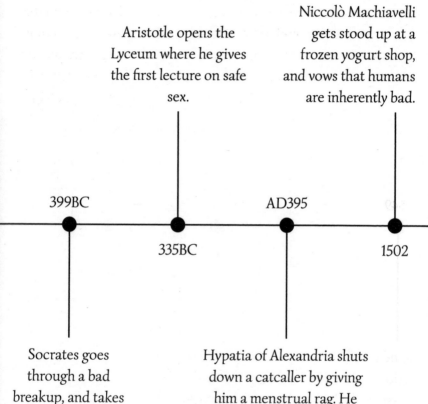

Aristotle opens the Lyceum where he gives the first lecture on safe sex.

Niccolò Machiavelli gets stood up at a frozen yogurt shop, and vows that humans are inherently bad.

399BC

AD395

335BC

1502

Socrates goes through a bad breakup, and takes some hemlock.

Hypatia of Alexandria shuts down a catcaller by giving him a menstrual rag. He does not bother her again.

Thomas Hobbes writes *Leviathan*, which argues for a social contract and an absolute sovereign to avoid civil war. He also happened to be going through a nasty divorce at the time.

Baruch Spinoza is banned from the Jewish community in Amsterdam after misbehaving on his birthright trip.

1649

1651

1651

1656

René Descartes writes the treatise *Passions of the Soul* to prove that he is capable of feeling emotion. No one believes him.

Anne marries the 1st Earl of Conway, mostly for his huge library.

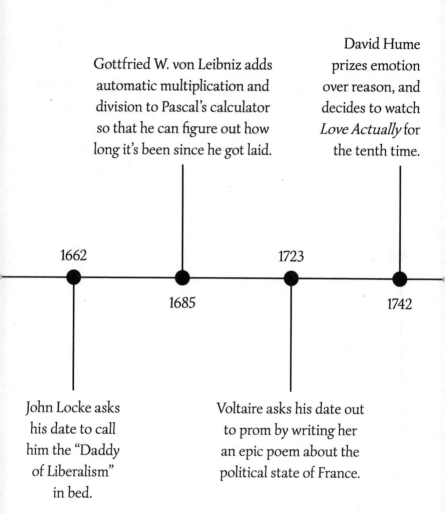

Gottfried W. von Leibniz adds automatic multiplication and division to Pascal's calculator so that he can figure out how long it's been since he got laid.

David Hume prizes emotion over reason, and decides to watch *Love Actually* for the tenth time.

1662

1685

1723

1742

John Locke asks his date to call him the "Daddy of Liberalism" in bed.

Voltaire asks his date out to prom by writing her an epic poem about the political state of France.

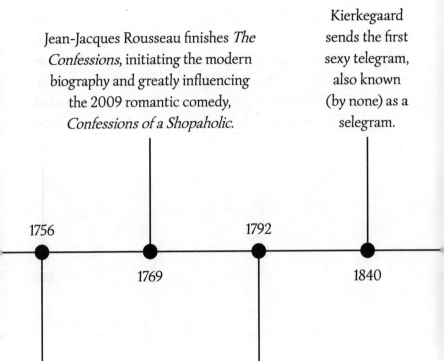

Jean-Jacques Rousseau finishes *The Confessions*, initiating the modern biography and greatly influencing the 2009 romantic comedy, *Confessions of a Shopaholic*.

Kierkegaard sends the first sexy telegram, also known (by none) as a selegram.

1756

1792

1769

1840

Immanuel Kant accidentally double-books two dates at once, and has his first moral crisis.

Mary Wollstonecraft publishes *A Vindication of the Rights of Woman* after starring in *The Vagina Monologues* in college.

Karl Marx is so busy
getting exiled from
Paris that he forgets his
five-year anniversary.
He is promptly exiled
from the bedroom.

Nietzsche gets
acne before a big
date and decides
that God is dead.

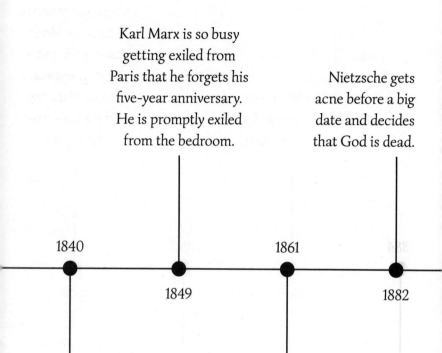

1840

1861

1849

1882

Margaret Fuller becomes
the first editor of *The
Dial* and organizes
"conversations" with
women to compensate
for the lack of access
to education. She is
the Carrie Bradshaw of
transcendentalism.

John Stuart Mill
recovers from a
breakup by writing
the ultimate self-help
book, *Utilitarianism*.

Carl Jung admits to having extramarital relationships, but explains that it's only because he's still figuring out his collective unconscious.

W.E.B. Du Bois co-founds the NAACP and is declared Sexiest Man Alive.

1884

1909

1912

1916

Freud brings his date cocaine for Valentine's Day. Although hesitant at first, she trusts Freud's medical opinion and agrees to try some. She is soon addicted to cocaine.

Ludwig Wittgenstein finds both language and the conception of sexuality too confining.

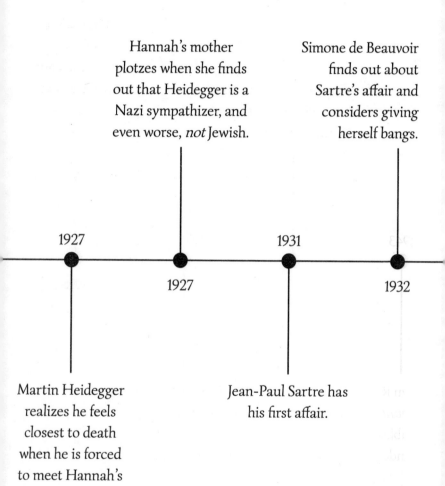

Hannah's mother plotzes when she finds out that Heidegger is a Nazi sympathizer, and even worse, *not* Jewish.

Simone de Beauvoir finds out about Sartre's affair and considers giving herself bangs.

1927

1927

1931

1932

Martin Heidegger realizes he feels closest to death when he is forced to meet Hannah's parents.

Jean-Paul Sartre has his first affair.

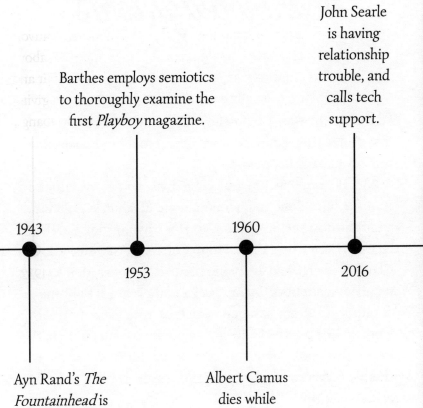

John Searle is having relationship trouble, and calls tech support.

Barthes employs semiotics to thoroughly examine the first *Playboy* magazine.

1943

1960

1953

2016

Ayn Rand's *The Fountainhead* is published. Her Tinder bio just reads: "Greatest writer of all time. We can lie about how we met if it's in your best interest."

Albert Camus dies while sexting and driving.

Acknowledgments

I'd like to thank the following people, who fearlessly read first drafts, listened to me worry about fonts and made sure this book really happened:

Nira Begum, I feel so grateful to have you as my editor. I couldn't have done this without your invaluable guidance and reassuring emails. Thank you for trusting me enough to let me write a whole book. Philip Cotterell, Andrew Furlow, Claire Maxwell, and everyone else at Icon Books, thank you for all your support. Shara Zaval and the team at Publishers Group West, I am so appreciative of your help and hard work on this project. Hallie Bateman, for collaborating with me on this book and creating such incredible illustrations. Connie Gabbert, for designing the cover. James Tattle, for thinking of the brilliant title.

Emma Allen, for publishing the original article in *The New Yorker*. Erin "Übermensch" Liu, not only are you one of the greatest philosophers of our time but also a beautiful and generous friend. Sophie Tupholme and Sarah MacArthur, for sitting with me in Blanc de Blanc while we waited for our laundry to dry and tried to think of what rhymed with 'tabula rasa' (not a lot, it turns out). Everyone at Meathaus, thank you for taking me in off the streets of Long Island. Sam Hoffman, for being my first husband and friend. Maria Yagoda, Ainhoa Hardy, and Chiara Gerek, for keeping me going. Amanda Abrams, my best friend and favorite dentist, thank you for constantly yelling at me to sit down and write this book and then distracting me five minutes later. I love you.

Papa, thank you for always listening, and Aaron and Sammy, for being there. Mom, thank you for your unequivocal love, friendship and encouragement. You gave me life so here is this acknowledgments page, I hope we are even now. Barbara, you always know what to wear and who to call. Monique et Maurice, Grandma and Grandpa, I wouldn't be here without you. Je vous aime. John Searle and Slavoj Žižek, thank you for taking the time to contribute original entries. I feel honored to have your words beside mine. Finally, to all the philosophers who inspired, taught and entertained me, I know you probably wish you weren't included in a book that uses the phrases "hand-job" and "categorical imperative" in the same sentence. I'm sorry.